MW00901456

DIY Business Plan
That Works

A Layman's Step By Step Guide to Creating Your Own Business Plan A to Z

(Downloadable Templates)

By

Robert R. Stimson

Lost River
Publishing House

Cover design

Mary Perez

First Edition

CONTENTS

INTRODUCTION

Do you think business plans are difficult to write? Too dull, and long? Not worthwhile and useless? Did you roll your eyes just looking at the Table of Contents of this book?

Maybe you have tried writing a business plan yourself. Failed or gave up. You've heard the moans, groans, and complaints of others going through the process of writing a business plan.

Fear no longer. I will teach you that fear, dread and misunderstanding do not have to come into it.

I speak from experience. I will share my knowledge, and the knowledge of other successful business people, in this book. With over 30 years of business experience, I have written many winning business plans over that time.

I have written business plans as an entrepreneur, adjusted plans as a business owner to expand my business. I have initiated business plans for corporate services that didn't exist at the time.

Each business plan I wrote resulted in thriving operations, as well as, profitable new corporate products and services. The plans were fully complete, official business plans. But, slimmed down from the scary 40 to 100-pages of olden times.

More than likely you will think of your business, maybe outline it in your head, talk about it with some friends. Next, you'll write down what you know today.

Determine what you need to research and learn. Write your first draft. Then change it. After a reality check, you will need more research and industry, marketing or customer information. Then change it again.

Knowing this process up front will help keep you from getting frustrated. This is just how it works. All you have to do is plan in advance and give yourself plenty of time to write the best plan ever. From this book, you will learn what to write and how to write it.

I can, however, let you know right now that after you go through the process of writing, changing and finally finishing your business plan, it will be wrong the minute you print it out.

Can you guess why? Because some things are beyond your control, but still affect you and your business on a daily basis. You cannot control an industry change or a consumer change

Here you will learn to jump all the hurdles and reach success with an A+ business plan that makes your business work for you.

WHAT IS A BUSINESS PLAN?

You will hear and read any variations of the following:

- Simply, a guide and roadmap that states your business goals and how you will accomplish those goals.

- A business plan tells who you are, what business you want to start or expand, and to offer proof that you can do it and how.

- A road map, a benchmark. A written plan of operational, financial and marketing viewpoints.

- A written document detailing what sets you apart and makes you unique or special. What is your motive, the funding required, and what's in it for the investors?

- A written description of your business's future. What are you going to do, and how will you accomplish it?

- A plan will provide answers to a comprehensive list of various, vital questions for multiple audiences.

These are correct, but is that it? Simply this, only that? Audiences, a road map, motives? Put that in plain English.

A business plan is your company's resume.

When you write your draft and start your plan, think of your resume. How often have you changed or reorganized your resume? Are your accomplishments precise and appropriate for the job?

Have you written your resume to highlight specific titles and duties? Does your resume state your experience so that it justifies your best salary opportunity?

We can compare your resume to a business plan:

- ✓ Your resume defines who you are and what you do.
- ✓ Your business plan defines what your business is and what it will do.

- ✓ Your resume defines your accomplished goals and strategy.
- ✓ Your business plan defines business goals and strategies for success.

- ✓ Your resume is explicitly written to the job you are applying for.
- ✓ Your business plan is specific to your product and target market.

- ✓ Your resume identifies the benefits, opportunities, and experience you have which can successfully resolve problems the employer is looking to solve.

- ✓ Your business plan identifies your business opportunities, and strategy to foresee and resolve potential problems.

- ✓ Your resume reflects you and your ability to think, organize and communicate.
- ✓ Your business plan reflects you and the management team's ability to think through and revise a plan and have a specific strategy for communications.

- ✓ Your resume conveys your aptitude for contributing to the success of a company justifying the upper scale of salaries offered.
- ✓ Your business plan conveys your aptitude for success and shows investors your ability to compete in your industry and produce profits.

A business plan is your company's definition and the reason for being.

Your business plan is an explanation of the business you want, the product or service you want to sell. It is a plan of your goals for growing the company, your ability to make a profit. It clearly defines your strategy for accomplishing those goals through marketing, sales and extensive knowledge of your industry.

HOW CRITICAL IS A BUSINESS PLAN?

Do you really need a business plan? Yes. The only person who doesn't need a business plan is someone who is not starting or expanding a business.

Without a business plan, how do you intend to outline your business ideas and goals? Where will you state what you are going to do and how? How will you describe who you are? Will you be able to detail how much money you need and where the money will be spent?

What information will you use to forecast how your business will look in the next year to three years? How will you clearly and professionally develop your organization and management? How will you keep track of and test your market research and analysis?

Your business plan is the basis of your funding proposal. Your request, in the form of a business plan, is submitted to your financial community so that you can obtain the funding you need to start or expand your business.

Your plan is the vital instrument used to obtain capital. And, it is equally important to help you align internal goals with market demand on an ongoing basis.

Start your new business without a business plan?
You are doomed to fail.

Don't muck around. This is your living we are talking about. Even if you are just planning a part-time business, you need a plan to detail your own goals, a work schedule, and determine how much an hour you need to make.

In an in-home business or part-time situation, you may only need a one-page or what is known as a lean business plan. If you choose either of these formats, it is imperative to outline the direction you want to take your business and drive a stake into the goals you want to accomplish in order to make money.

Without a traditional plan, a one-page plan or at least a summary, you may have some success. But your chances of failing are scientifically higher.

A study in *The Journal of Business Venturing* states that over 11,000 companies that developed a business plan overall improved their business performance. That same study also found that planning significantly benefits existing companies.

A *Journal of Management* study states that companies who write business plans grow thirty percent faster than companies that don't. This study also points out that businesses can be successful without planning. However, a company starting with a business plan grows faster and enjoys more success than those without.

To reinforce the connection between planning and success, another study implemented by the *Journal of Small Business Management* "found that fast-growing companies--meaning companies with over ninety-two percent growth in sales from one year to the next—usually have business plans.

If you are reading this book, you are either ready to write a business plan, just checking out what is involved in writing a plan, or looking for a reason not to write one.

When you get to the chapters in this book where I outline every section included in a business plan, you will clearly see the importance of one.

HERE ARE 5 UNDENIABLE REASONS YOU NEED A BUSINESS PLAN

A BUSINESS PLAN IS MANDATORY FOR BUSINESSES SEEKING FINANCING

- Presentation to a financial institution.
- Pitching a business idea to investors.
- Applying for a small business grant.
- Petitioning for the support of a business partner.

All potential investors will require you to show them the true potential of your business and the only acceptable way to clearly detail hard facts and numbers.

A BUSINESS PLAN HELPS YOU MAKE DECISIONS

There are chapters or sections in a traditional business plan you are unable to write if you are undecided or not committed to your product, service or even the idea of starting a new business.

Completing your business plan eliminates any gray areas. For instance, say that you are not exactly sure about the configuration of the product or service you want to sell. Therefore, you don't know the price point.

A BUSINESS PLAN GIVES YOU NEW IDEAS

Writing your business plan opens up new kinds of ideas, it offers learning potential, opens up ideas for experimentation and fresh perspectives. You may discover a different approach than the one you started with.

Forget the bad reputation of business plans, as I covered in the Introduction. Don't let your plan be the old-time long, boring, hard to read and hard to follow rigid document. Create your business plan as a growing, evolving, dynamic and flexible business tool.

A BUSINESS PLAN IS A REALITY CHECK

You want to blast-off a new business but have not stopped to think if your plan is too short on information, or if it includes unsubstantiated information.

Have you worked up a mock-up or samples of your product to test or show to people? Do you have information gathered from outside opinions or focus groups regarding the feasibility of your product or service?

Can you prove that someone will actually buy your product or service at your price point? Do your financials prove it? This kind of questioning may scare some people. Not knowing if the plan is underdeveloped, how to figure it out, or how to fix it puts you on shaky ground.

You can eliminate this frustration by identifying gaps early on in the writing process. If the plan, or your vision of the product, does not pass the reality check, use this opportunity to strengthen and expand your research. Conduct additional testing of your ideas and/or product proving the business plan viable.

A BUSINESS PLAN IS ALSO YOUR ACTION PLAN

Your business plan lays out your actions, next steps, future growth and your strategies for meeting your goals.

This sets your benchmark for the beginning of your startup. It states and proves where you are starting from, the action plan for moving forward, and the directions to get there.

If at any point in time, you ask yourself what you are doing, where are you and where should you go, get your plan off the shelf and get your business back on target, or revamp the plan.

Ask me again if you need a business plan?

There's a smart guy named Sean Hackney.
He didn't want to start a business. But, he

wanted to persuade a soft drink company to hire him. So, he wrote a plan for a product that would take on his former employer, Red Bull North America, Inc.

After finishing his business plan, he took it to his corporate attorney, and former Red Bull North America, Inc. managing director.

At the meeting, Hackney recalls them saying, "Don't send this to Coke or Pepsi. Start the business, and we'll start it with you."

That was back in 2000. Today, he is the co-founder and co-owner of Roaring Lion Energy Drink, a $6. 2 million companies in Sun Valley, California.

Starting with an investment of $62,000 the business is now the No. 2 energy drink sold in bars and nightclubs.

The company now has 32 employees. The first business plan he wrote has gone through many revisions. Today, he and the other co-founders regularly update the marketing plan, which is a guide for running the company.

Hackney has said that writing that plan was absolutely worthwhile.

"I had a lot of stuff in my head that needed [to be] put on paper."

I know that big success stories will not happen for all of us. But, they are inspiring. Use them to think about the possibilities, and be creative. No matter how small the idea, no matter the success, a business plan keeps you focused.

WHO IS THE BUSINESS PLAN WRITTEN FOR?

- You.

- Your employees.

- Key personnel hires.

- Bankers, investors, venture capitalist (VC) or angel investors.

- Your business to use as a benchmark.

- Your family.

- Your company partner(s).

- Vendors who must understand your needs.

- Vendors who may want to be partners or investors.

Some groups may not need to see the entire plan, just select chapters or sub-sets. Otherwise, your business plan is a guarded secret.

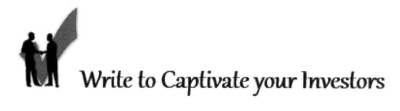
Write to Captivate your Investors

WHAT DO I WRITE AND HOW?

You are going to write an A+ business plan, based on the traditional sections of, and format of industrywide acceptable formats.

First, you need to learn and have a full understanding of the basic elements of a business plan. In the next chapter, I will cover the different acceptable formats you can choose.

Regardless of the format, you select, all of the elements must be included. The format and presentation may look different, but the information is the same.

Simply start writing your business plan from today. Adjust later.

First, open up your word processing software or get a yellow legal pad and pencil.

Use a separate piece of paper, or page, for each category, element, and chapter. These titles are interchangeable. This is free-writing only, so do not worry about the ifs, ands or buts, just yet.

You will begin with a 'brain dump.' Write down everything you know about your business idea by each section that is included in your plan. This free-write is a start toward writing your first draft.

This is a 'get your thoughts together' exercise. For instance, what do you know about your industry today? What do you know about running a business, about your product or service? How will you set up your organization?

Don't waste time waiting for all the answers. You will fill in information, fix gaps, polish and adjust your information as you learn more about your industry, the market, and your capabilities.

Big Tip

You <u>must</u> personally be familiar with all the information you provide in your business plan. As well as, having a full understanding of all rules, aspects and business ownership.

Here is what you are going to write, with a description of how. You should choose one writing format and be consistent throughout the document.

Each page represents a separate section with a specific purpose.

1. EXECUTIVE SUMMARY

Write this section last. You don't have enough information today to draft a concise executive summary. But here are some ideas to keep in mind.

This is the overall summary of the detailed information in your plan. Here you tell the investors everything. It is a selling tool, and it needs to grab the reader.

As you go from no information to writing drafts, it may help to know how a journalist writes a story. The answers are always provided for each of the following questions: who, what, where, when, why and how.

These are the questions your executive summary will summarize.

2. COMPANY DESCRIPTION

What service(s) and/or product(s) you will offer as you know them today?

For example, what is your business? How will you conduct business? Will you be a sole proprietor, LLC, other partnership or corporation? You might be a 'doing business as' (DBA). Do you need office and storage space, or office only? Lease? Plans for owning?

Will you have a board of directors, advisory board, company or corporate secretary or advisers. Will they get paid? Are you planning to go public sometime in the future? If so, when.

What licenses or other regulations do you have to satisfy? What is your mission statement? Will you have a vision statement or both?

3. PRODUCT/SERVICE DESCRIPTION

A detailed explanation of the service or product your business will sell. Tell what you have developed. Do you have a model, sample or mock-up to show your investors or interested parties? What makes your product unique? What problem does your product or service solve and how? How will you produce and distribute your product or service?

4. MARKET ANALYSIS

Explain your market and define your target market. Identify your customers with the demographic and psychographic profiles needed to explain and prove who your customers are. What is the demand for your product or service? Any foreseeable changes? What are your competitors doing?

How deep is your market and how far out will you go to reach it? What is happening in the industry? What is happening with population shifts? For instance, a big migration to Florida, uncertain movement in California, a big loss of population in the Rust Belt? Specific ethnic pockets in your city?

5. MARKETING AND ADVERTISING CHANNELS

How will you sell your product? What is your plan of attack to reach your target market? What are your plans to reach various segments of your market, and through what means?

Is your product or service geared to businesses and corporations? Small businesses? Corporate division sections such as management, information technology, HR, sales? What advertising channels will you use?

What are your plans for various types of media advertising for each segment of your target market? Which social media will be a sales channel?

Describe your overall plan of attack to capture your market.

6. MANAGEMENT STRUCTURE

You will be the key man/woman. Eventually, you will need key man insurance. Who else will be part of the management team?

What will be the chain of command? What are the resumes and experience required for management personnel?

There are taxes to be filed and bookkeeping. Are those functions going to be a management job?

Are the co-founders going to be included in day-to-day functions? What are the titles and duties of your management team?

7. OPERATING PLAN

This is the section where you get down into the day-to-day running of the business. Cover areas like production, manufacturing if suitable, inventory and distribution.

You are not addressing theory or concepts, but putting down how you will make a product, store it, and disburse it. Of course, this varies by the kind of business you want to start, but here you face the details suitable to your business.

8. FINANCIAL PLAN

How much money do you need? How will you spend the investor's money? Are you contributing any capital? What do finances look like for the next year? What is the financial goal for profits the first year? What is the plan for the next three years?

What are your expenses? What overhead, cost of the product or service, equipment, manufacturing, wholesale buys, and how much revenue will you have to generate to cover all expenses? When will you break-even?

9. REQUEST FOR FUNDING

What are your funding options?
Write your request geared to those specific audiences.

The questions and descriptions in each category above, are examples of the information to be included in each segment. They represent a place to start while you research and learn the additional information needed for your plan.

You must personally know your business backward and forward, like the back of your hand. Who can do the best job to get you prepared to sit in front of a room full of investors or bankers? You!

By now you have finished your free-write exercise and can identify additional information needed. Such as research, testing, reality checks, etc. We are ready for the next steps, but first I want to remind you of some valuable information to use while you write your first, second or third draft.

- Reduce some of the pressure by reminding yourself that you do not have to write the whole plan all at once, straight through to the end.

- Continue breaking the plan down by each chapter in the business plan.

- Continue to improve each chapter, individually. Later on, you can share, or repeat small amounts of information, from one section to another.

- Consider the executive summary structure as a who, what, where, when, why, and how.

- Reality checks are a must.
- Designate milestones to perform reality checks. Milestones within writing your plan, i.e., meet your own deadlines. And milestones you plan to reach in the business as stated in the plan.

- If you need to make changes and adjustments after the reality check, you may feel as though you are going backward. You are not. The payoff is a stronger, more viable plan.

- From the reality check, determine the gaps you need to fill in, correct or adjust, by individual chapter. This could mean performing additional testing of your product, adding new data to substantiate what you have written or a rewrite with more clarity.

- A number of things can show up at any time. Therefore, each subsequent rewrite will include the additional information and data you discovered during your reality checks.

- If you print out your drafts, put the date and the time they were printed on each one. This keeps various copies of drafts in order, eliminating mix-ups.

You learned sentence structure, placement, and how paragraphs support the main thought in English Composition class. Here is a reminder, even though the format may not fit all chapters since you will be providing charts and graphs for some of those.

- Typical composition form teaches first to free-write, the 'brain dump.' The free-write exercise we covered earlier. The goal is to put what you know and think down on paper.

- Organize the draft of each chapter. An outline helps to identify critical information and serves as a check to make sure you have included every detail you want to discuss. The use of outlines is significant.

- The most important sentence is the first one, in the very first paragraph under each heading, or chapter, of your plan.

- In that first paragraph or introduction to that chapter, you state your premise for that topic.

- The paragraphs that follow the first one build on each other to support or validate your premise.

- You must substantiate each premise with no less than three supporting points. You can write as many supporting paragraphs as you need, but at least three for every premise.

- You can include multiple suppositions, or premises, in each segment.

- Each point or premise has to be supported by proof and logical thinking.

For example, the proof is explained with industry research, history of industry trends, citing real case examples, history of customer behavior, quotes and/or opinions from reliable sources, and specific facts. Results of testing your product or service. Logic is, 'Well, does all of this make sense?'

- In summary, the first paragraph of the chapter states your premise. The next three-five paragraphs provide proof and logic that substantiate that premise.

- The final paragraph of the chapter, the premise or section is the conclusion.

TWO BEST PRACTICES IN BUSINESS PLAN WRITING

A discussion about writing your business plan, would not be complete without outlining 'best practices.'

Every business venture should observe what is called in the business world 'best practices.' They are:

1. You must write the plan yourself. It seems like hard work and takes a lot of effort on your part. But, it pays off in the end. You will hear me say it over: you must know your business plan and industry like the back of your hand.

Know your industry, first for yourself so you can identify management tactics and goals. Second, for investors. If you do not universally know your industry, doors will be closed in your face.

You are expected to thoroughly explain the type of business you are in or want to start up. Bankers and investors want to clearly understand the nature of your business, the state of the industry, its history, and future and be assured that you know it.

This means knowing the competitors in your industry. You will need to detail distribution configurations, confidently discuss your competition, their buying partners, and the share of the market they hold.

Everything within your industry happens outside of your business. In other words, anything out there could affect your company at any minute. So, in essence, the more you know, the better your advantage and strategy will be.

2. The second component of exercising best practices in writing your business plan is to use the plan you write. Again, use the plan you write. Don't just put it in a file drawer and think that is the end of it. I will keep saying that you need to use your plan to run your business. It has to be reviewed and updated and adjusted no less than every quarter end.

You write the plan, adjust it, change it and analyze it. Rewrite it, then do it all again. Everything that happens in the industry even while you are writing your plan affects your business. A competitor will be glad to steal your customers at any time.

Some changes are beyond your control and your plan changes because of those circumstances. Your goals may change. Therefore, your business plan changes with those goals as well as with your company's growth or decline.

A competitor opens up before you in the proximity of your desired location. A new product similar to yours hits the market before yours. The lady next door has a jump on opening a retail store, interior design, or as a business consultant.

Keep in mind that you may also have to make changes in production, location, implementation, distribution channels, and changes in customer demand. Or, any adjustments required by your investors.

Scary Tip
Your plan is wrong the day you print it.

I've mentioned this before. But, let me explain. I'm not saying your business plan is wrong in the sense that you did not do it correctly from the outset.

The terminology means that the second you finish your plan, something has changed in the market. Circumstances beyond your control.

It is an evolving, open-ended living document. So, by definition, it cannot stay static.

Somewhere along the line a term you may come across is the business model. A business model is your revenue and expense detail. The business model is 'How are you going to make money?'

"A business model lays out a step-by-step plan of action for profitably operating the business in a specific marketplace. The business model for a restaurant is significantly different from the business model for an online business for instance.

"... A business model should also include projected startup costs and sources of financing, the target customer base for the business, marketing strategy, competition, and projections of revenues and expenses. One of the most common mistakes leading to the failure of business startups is a failure to project the necessary expenses to fund the business to the point of profitability, i.e., the point in time when revenues exceed expenses.

"If possible, a business model should include any possible plans for partnering with other existing businesses. An example of this would be an advertising business that aims to establish an arrangement for referrals to and from a printing company."

Another term you may come across is **a value proposition**. It is a concise statement of what your business will offer in product or services. In other words, what value, or issue are you bringing to a customer to resolve his or her problem. The term also includes the difference between your company and your competitors.

The statement from Investitopia continues by saying, "Even if two businesses operate within the same industry, they likely have different competitive advantages and disadvantages and, therefore, need different business models."

When you find various terms used to describe the same things. It is okay. Just be sure to stay consistent. Pick a term… stay with it!

WHAT KIND OF BUSINESS PLAN SHOULD I WRITE?

When Abraham Lincoln was asked how long his legs were, he said, "… as long as they need to be!"

Therefore, you know when you have not given enough information, while you suspect your weakest points.

There are many styles and lengths of business plans for you to implement. A business plan can be started just about anywhere, on anything.

****

There is a legend about two friends. Rollin King was a banker and a pilot for a small charter airline. Herb Kelleher was an attorney.

In 1966, in a San Antonio bar, they had a conversation that led to an idea for an airline. Offering low cost, short, intrastate flights.

After mapping out routes, the kernel of their business plan was a triangle on a cocktail napkin. The triangle on that cocktail napkin was the beginning of Southwest Airlines.

****

Few celebrities can enjoy first-name recognition such as Oprah Winfrey. Ho⋯ ⋯me wouldn't have the power it has today if sh⋯ ⋯been persuaded to syndicate her media interest

Oprah ⋯ ⋯bating whether or not to syndicate with ABC.

While having a meal with film critic Robert Ebert and discussing
the syndicate idea, Ebert used a table napkin and ballpoint pen and drew out some simple calculations.

Oprah's media empire is now worth $2.9 billion.

****

While a student and researcher at both the University of Pittsburgh and the Mellon Institute of Industrial Research, chemist Paul Lauterbur brainstormed his idea for the MRI.

In the 1970s Lauterbur was eating at a suburban Pittsburgh hamburger place, Big Boys. He drafted his MRI design on table napkins.

Three decades later he won a Nobel Prize.

****

I am not saying that we all need to hang out in bars and restaurants with table napkins and pens at the ready. I am not saying that we will win a Noble Prize or end up with a $2.9 billion empire.

To put it in perspective, what I am saying is that in each of these cases a business plan of some kind was needed, initiated, expanded on, and implemented with success.

The types of business plans accepted in the current business arena are the Traditional Business Plan and the Lean Business Plan.

As an example of which plan to use, a new profit center for a corporation requires a traditional plan. It needs specifics detailing how the new profit center works within the existing company. How it will get built and a description of the benefits.

The same kind of full-blown traditional plan is used for a new business startup and/or an extension to an existing business.
The length of a business plan is mostly governed by who you are approaching for funding. The bank, angel investor, VC, etc. dictate how much information you need to include.

The Lean Plan is in a summary format, chart or bullet point one-pager.

Some examples of a lean plan are an Avon lady, dog walker, delivery service, massage therapist, plus any small business that can be run out of your home. Maybe an attorney is simply renting an office. A one-pager should suffice for your benefit if you are not looking for outside funding.

As stated, I am going to go through the lean business plan and the traditional business plan with you in the following chapters. Your job is to get the data together, pick a style of plan, stick with it and be consistent.

LEAN BUSINESS PLAN VERSUS TRADITIONAL BUSINESS PLAN

Lean	Traditional
Strategy	
Business model or canvas	Business Plan
Theory-driven	Application-driven
New Product Process	
Owner/Partner development development	Product management
Test concept out of the office	Outline a step-by-step plan
New Product Development	
Fast development	Agile or waterfall development
Quick changes, involving repetition first	Build theory of product, or specs
Organization	
Owner/Partner	Departments by function
Hire for fast learners with quick of	Hire for experience and strength
turn-around skills	management skills
Financial Reporting	
Quantitative numbers	Accounting cash flow reports
Target market acquisition cost	Balance sheets, P&L
Overhead	
Failure	
Expected	Exception
Fix by adjusting ideas and abandon	Fix by firing executives

Failed iterations

Quick	Measured
Uses 'good-enough' data	Requires more complex data

THE LEAN BUSINESS PLAN

The lean business plan is an elevated focus, including only key elements. It doesn't mean slacker or looser; it means shorter. What does lean mean? A concise, strong, no-frills plan.

It is a set of beliefs based on plan-run-review-revise. It was first put into play about seventy years ago to accomplish lean manufacturing. By Toyota, specifically.

The plan can be written using bullets, tables, charts, lists or Excel worksheets. It is used as a check on company goals, tells how you will run the process, set expectations and define accountability. Review it monthly to track your progress and determine any adjustments.

For a lean plan or one-page business plan, the extensive, big deal executive summary is not needed. So, whether you are writing a lean plan or a one-page plan, those pages, or page *is* the executive summary.

Think of it as a 'pitch.' Whatever you want to call it, it has specific points of information that must be included. To get started, gather all of the information about the following and start writing.

1. What is the specific problem your customer has? What problems do you want to solve?

2. Describe how your product or service solves the consumers' problem(s).

3. How will you operate, what are your costs and how much time will you dedicate to the business each day? In other words, **how will you make money?**

4. Who is your target market? In #1 and #2, you wrote what the customers' problem(s) are and how you will fix them. So, here in #4 answer who is your customer? Who are you fixing the problem for?

   You have to do research because in addition to identifying your target market, you must know the potential size of that market and if there is enough money to be made from those target customers.

   Find out what you have that no one else has? Does someone else not have the resources you have, or are they too small or too inconsistent to get the job done?

   Can you do it better, cheaper? How are you unique? Clearly state and discuss your competitive advantage.

5. Who is going to run your business? Just you, a friend or family member pitching in? Who is ultimately responsible for the management of the company?

6. Include a financial summary. How much is it going to cost to run the business? How much does product or equipment cost? Where will you be based? Your home, borrowed space, garage?

    What supplies are needed? Will you have part-time help? Make a full list with dollar costs. The company has to pay all overhead.

7. Identify where the money is coming from. How much money is needed? Are you going to pay as you go just scratching by as you can? How does that affect your monthly home budget?

    Will you be able to handle any personal or business surprises? Are you just going to work part-time until business picks up? What is your commitment to the business' financial health?

    Are you raising the money, using savings, cashing in an individual retirement account? How will you pay for any early withdrawal penalty fees? Are you borrowing it? Using credit cards? What is the dollar amount needed to get this business started, up and running? Through break-even to profit making.

All of this information plus your knowledge develops your strategy. After a draft(s), you can determine the headings, format, and information you want to use in the plan.

Remember that a plan is a living and evolving thing. So, include how and when you will review and revise the plan. What strategy you will use for the continuous improvement of your business and increased profits.

The lean plan is for your use, use whatever title or format that is best for you. Just be consistent. The plan does not have to be daunting. Start simple, let it develop organically, and keep each element succinct.

Everything written must have a business purpose. If you are not using the lean plan for fundraising, you don't need as much detail. Such as an extensive write-up on management; resumes, background, exit strategy, etc.

EXAMPLE OF A ONE-PAGE LEAN PLAN IN CHART FORM, FOR A CAR WASH SERVICE

Simon Says Wash Your Car	

Identity/Business Strategy	
We offer a high-quality mobile car wash and detailing at your location.	

Problem to Solve	Our Solution
It's hard to find time to keep your car clean, detailed and protected from the weather.	Simon Says is your car care expert. We provide a luxury wash and full detail to your car.

Target Market	Competition
Working and stay at home men, women and families.	Car washes, dealership repair garages

Sales Channel	Marketing Tactics
We sell our services through gas stations, gyms, fast lunch close to large working city areas.	Partner with gyms, gas stations, restaurants. Have businesses display flyers and HR to offer company discounts.

Revenue	Expenses	
1. Car wash only 2. Car wash and detail	Truck, retrofit Water or supply Wax Armor All Rags	Office supplies Tire brushes Grease remover Buckets Insurance

Milestones	
Q1 budget	**Distribute Flyers**
(Joe, Dec. 15)	Contact businesses
	(Jan. 12)
Build a website	
Contract	**Compile a list of advertisers**
(Jan. 20)	(Jan, Feb. 22)

Team	Partners, Resources
Joe, Owner	Joe, Tom, Partners
Jan, Advertising and appointment setting	
	Personal funds
Joe, Tom	Small business loan
Workers	

Details for Each Section of the Charted Lean Business Plan

Following is a breakdown of each section of the lean business plan example.

IDENTITY/BUSINESS STRATEGY

Your business strategy is to identify and focus on the target market with a problem to solve. And, match those customers up with your products or services that solve that problem. Simply state the problem and how you will solve it.

We offer high-quality mobile car wash and detailing at your location.

THE PROBLEM, SOLUTION, FUNDING

Problem to Solve	Our Solution
It is hard to find time to keep your car clean, detailed	Simon Says is your car care expert. We provide
and protected from the weather.	a luxury wash and full detail for your car.
Funding	Owners, or small personal loan

Begin with a couple of short sentences or bullet points. Here, the Simon Says the problem is that people do not always have enough extra time to keep their cars clean and protected from the weather.

Simon's solution is to go to the customer's location and get the job done without loss of any time to the customer.

You must have a solution to a problem. Not a solution hunting for a problem. It does not make sense, does it? If your product or services do not solve a problem or an issue than you are pushing a boulder up a hill.

TARGET MARKET AND COMPETITION

Target Market	Competition
Working and stay at home men, women and families.	Car washes, dealerships

You need market research to determine your competitors. For instance, a do-it-yourself car wash or drive through car wash and detail. Your immediate need is to find an area and a way to test your business idea.

Everyone is busy. How big is that target market? Simon knows that it is huge, has to figure out where his biggest group of customers are, and how big a chunk of the business he can capture.

Think: Who is my ideal customer? What are their fundamental characteristics?

At this point, Simon Says he knows that his target is the people who work away from home in offices, and other businesses.

Other markets are people who do not work outside of their home but manage the family and house. Additionally, people who work from home, i.e., run a business from their home office.

SALES STRATEGY

Sales Channel	Marketing Tactics
We sell our services through gas stations, gyms, fast lunch places close to large working centers. Repair garages, mall parking lots.	Partner with gyms, gas stations, restaurants. Have businesses display flyers and HR to offer company discounts.

What is your sales strategy to put your product or service out in the market? Are you going old school 'feet on the ground'; a one-man sales force, high-tech? Are you selling online, social media? In other words, state how you will sell your product or service and what marketing and advertising strategy are in your arsenal.

A critical marketing 'must do' is for the owners' and staff cars to always look like they have just been washed and detailed. The same kind of clothing gives a unified feel. For instance, white polo shirts and khaki shorts. Clean white training shoes and socks.

BUSINESS MODEL

Revenue	Expenses	
		Office
1. Car wash only	Truck, retrofit	supplies
		Tire
2. Car wash and detail	Water or supply	brushes
	Wax	Grease remover
	Armor All	Buckets
	Rags	Insurance

How are you going to make money? Identify what it is going to take to get the job done. No 'pie-in-the-sky' forecasts. Your target market may not be as big as you think it is.

You need a revenue stream. But, if your business is only successful with a huge number of customers, you need to review pricing versus expenses, schedules, and time frames. You may need outside funding, or you may need a new idea.

In this example, Simon Says is offering an á la carte menu. Based on budget and the amount of available time, a customer can buy a car wash only. Or, a car wash with a detailing package.

Simon might discover when he tests his service that he needs to change the menu of services. For instance, a car wash only; a car wash and inside cleaning; or a car wash and full detail.

Simon can identify initial expenses, which may change during the testing stage. For instance, to get a truck and retrofit it for a car washing business is expensive. Can one be rented? Is there another way to achieve this? Simon's owner could find out he needs a protective canopy for shade. Or, to add window tinting to the business at some time to reinvent the service. Simon Says may already have the other supplies on hand. Forms could be made upon the PC or supplement them from an office supply store.

SCHEDULE

Identify what has to be done, how long it will take and schedule every step you know of that has to be completed.

Milestones	
Q1 budget	**Distribute Flyers**
(Joe, Dec. 15)	Contact businesses
	(Jan. 12)
Build a website	
Contract	**Compile a list of advertisers**
(Jan. 20)	(Jan, Feb. 22)

In this example, Joe is putting together the first quarter budget. Not necessarily in December, the business may start in the middle of a quarter. Use the dates for your own plan.

The budget is the first milestone for Simon Says. Getting flyers prepared and distributed, building a list of advertisers and completion of the website or social media content are other milestones.

Another milestone that Simon Says should have is when to test and make revisions. Should he test before the website is built? Before distributing flyers? What schedule would you put together?

I would not recommend spending a lot of money until I tested my service. Drafting a flyer and compiling a list of places to advertise doesn't cost anything and can be done in the planning stages.

Of course, you need at least a draft of your budget. Once you test your product or service you will have a budget on-hand to question, review and revise.

YOUR TEAM AND PARTNERS

Team	Partners, Resources
Joe, Owner	Joe, Tom, Partners
Jan, Advertising and appointment setting	Personal funds
Joe, Tom	Small business loan
Workers and	
Contractor	

Who is going to grow your business? At Simon Says, what key people are needed to effectively execute a tactical plan?

Joe, the owner, runs the business. He puts the plan together, figures out logistics and finds the money. More than likely, Joe will determine what the advertising will say, which printed ads might be used and where, and what events to attend.

Jan may be a part-time worker, a work from home helper, a family member, a temp. Jan will implement and distribute flyers, compose a list of places to advertise and set appointments.

In the beginning, Tom may have to start with voicemail and callbacks to set appointments. In the plan, that function will evolve as the business changes and grows.

For now, Joe and Tom are the working partners. They will do the testing and evaluation together. For a while, they may be the only employees. And, the only car washers.

The contract worker will build a website or develop the social media channels.

The same contract worker may be able to develop other print advertisements for Jan to place. Or, a different type of contractor may be needed. For instance, graphic artist, layout work, etc.

Where will Joe and Tom get the needed financing? They could use credit cards, savings, retirement money or loans from friends or family. Later they plan to take out a small business loan to build the business. For instance, two trucks, two paid employees, etc.

The lean business plan must include the process of tests, regular evaluations, and revisions. Joe and Tom will have to keep the business plan alive in order to generate profits, make changes and grow with the market.

Tracking progress, testing and revising is managing the business. Unexpected circumstances need to be handled, improvements made, and a continual comparison of the business plan to actual results.

Using these same details for writing a lean plan, extrapolate the information into a lean plan document that uses bullet points.

EXAMPLE OF A LEAN PLAN IN BULLET FORMAT FOR A CAR WASH SERVICE

Identity

Simon Says, Wash Your Car

Business Strategy

We offer high-quality mobile car wash and detailing services at your location.

Problem

- People's schedules today are so busy that most cannot find the time to wash, wax, detail or even clean out the inside of their cars. They are too busy or just don't want to do it.

Solution

- The company goes to the customer, appointments, and provides car washing packages at the customer's location.
- Funding

Target Market

- Working men and women.
- Stay at home individuals running and managing a household and family.

- Individuals who run a home-based business.

Competition

- Front yard, wash the car yourself.
- Professional car washes and detail businesses.
- Gas stations.
- Do-it-yourself drive in car washes.
- Dealerships.

Sales Channel

- Flyers
- Social media
- One-on-one sales
- Local publication's print ads
- Local events

Marketing Strategy

- Flyers at gas stations
- Punch cards at local gyms
- Flyer at lunch places at professional work areas or complexes
- Dealerships
- Shopping center parking lots

Business Model

Revenue

- Car wash only
- Car wash and interior clean

- Car wash with full detail

Expenses

- Truck
- Retrofit
- Water
- Wax and Armor All
- Rags, sponges, drying clothes
- Tire brushes
- Shampoo and grease remover
- Buckets/containers
- Office supplies
- Insurance

Milestones

Q1 budget	Joe	Dec. 15
Testing	Joe, Tom	Dec. 15 – Jan. 10
Revisions	Joe, Tom	Jan. 12
Build website	Contract	Jan. 18
Develop ads	Joe, Tom	Jan. 18
Develop flyers	Joe, Tom	Jan. 18
Develop punch cards	Joe, Tom	Jan. 18
Graphic works	Contract	Jan. 20
Printing	Jan	Jan. 22
List of advertisers	Jan	Jan. 20

Team

- Joe Simon

- Tom Simon
- Jan Smith
- Two Contractors

Partners

- Joe and Tom are equal sole proprietorship owners
- Joe and Tom fund the company in equal amounts

Resources

- Funds will come from, cash/liquid assets, savings, retirement funds, credit cards, friends, family.
- Funds will be used for all startup costs.
- Small business loan if necessary.

The example on the next page is called a Business Model Canvas. You can use this for a lean plan that goes beyond the type of home business we have been outlining.

Depending on what type of business you are opening you can use the following Business Model Canvas, either as a draft for a traditional plan or as a talking points sheet.

This could be a format for discussing your business idea with potential partners, mentors or even to test the waters with investors. You can use this for a lean plan for yourself.

The followin
outline the c

Business Model Canvas

EXAMPLE OF A VERY LEAN, NOT QUITE A COCKTAIL NAPKIN PLAN

From *www.Wikipedia.com*, here is a one-page, very informal business model canvas.

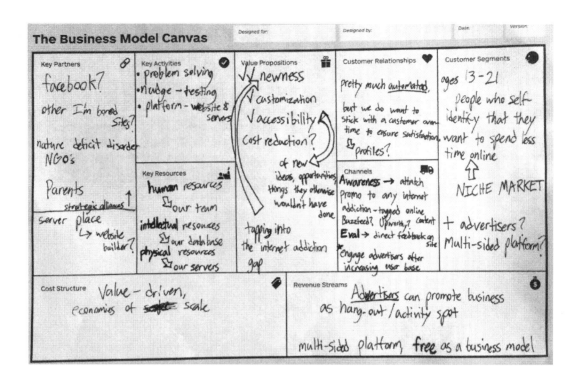

You could use something like this if it's only you, for example. Maybe you want to run a dog walking service or do Avon sales out of your home.

Any plan is better than no plan. Take your planning as seriously as you take your business. That being said, maybe this is all you need to work from.

TRADITIONAL BUSINESS PLAN

Your free writing exercise and outline is the best first draft of your traditional plan.

Today's traditional business plan is shorter than in previous days. More than likely it will be an online document or CD. You will still want to take a hard copy, or several, to any presentation meetings with investors.

Online copies can be sent as an attachment to the people who will be reviewing your funding request. Alternatively, your document can be emailed just to the head of the group, if requested, who will pass it on for their early discussion.

Ask how the investors want your face-to-face presentation. They may want a power point 'pitch' with handouts; a meeting in a casual setting with hard copies of the plan; or a screening conference call.

They may request hard copies and a straight-out oral presentation around a conference table. Always have hard copies available, and verify that equipment and outlets are available and work.

Whatever the case is, be prepared to review your plan with an audience. Let them ask questions about the information you present. Go immediately to the page that discusses that topic, have handouts for anticipated questions, or discuss orally.

Do not stand around and shuffle pages of paper or scroll through an entire power point to find the right place.

This is why it is imperative to know your business, industry and your business plan from front to back. You must be personally familiar with it.

COVER PAGE

The exact order of your chapters or topics is pretty standard. However, the cover page is always first, next is the executive summary, then the table of contents.

Here is a example of a basic cover page:

<u>**Business Plan**</u>

Name of Company

Address of Company
City, State, ZIP code

Telephone Number
Fax Number

Date of Plan Presentation

You may also include:

Presented to:
Name
Company

Name of Owner/Contact Person
Address
City, State, Zip
Telephone
Email

Here is the same page with adjustments:

Business Plan

Name of Company

Address of Company
City, State, ZIP code

Telephone Number
Fax Number

Somewhere in here add your logo and tagline if you have them.

Date of Plan Presentation

Date and number each revision: Oct. 23, 2018, Revision 2

Presented to:
Name
Company

If you include who you are presenting this plan to, remember to CHANGE THE NAME for the next presentation to investors.

CONFIDENTIAL

Name of

Owner/Contact Person

Telephone

Email

Number and extension if different from above

Your personal or business email

Website if you have it

Same page with changes at the bottom left:

Business Plan

Name of Company

Address of Company
City, State, ZIP code

Telephone Number
Fax Number

Somewhere in here add your logo and tagline if you have them.

Date of Plan Presentation

Presented to:
Name
Company

If you include who you are presenting this plan to, remember to CHANGE THE NAME for the next presentation to investors.

This is you. If the information is the same as company address, you can leave this out.

Name of Owner/Contact Person
Address
City, State, Zip
Telephone
Email

A simple example of a cover page that includes a confidentiality agreement. If you use this format, you must list the confidential agreement in the table of contents.

Business Plan

(Insert Date)

Company Name

▷▷▷ *A basic cover page. Add a larger company name and logo.*

Samples show this on the left and right side of the page, and sometimes change this information to a table of contents if it's short enough.

Principle ◁◁◁
Street address 1
Street address 2
City, state, ZIP |
Business phone
Website URL
Email address

Confidentiality Agreement

The undersigned acknowledges this any information provided by

_____

_____ in this business plan, or verbally, is

confidential and any disclosure may be detrimental to

_____.

Therefore, the undersigned agrees not to disclose any information without

express written permission from

_____.

If requested, the undersigned will ppromptly return this document to

_____

_____

Signature

_____

Name (Printed)

_____

Date

EXECUTIVE SUMMARY

The executive summary, two pages long, immediately follows your cover page. However, it is written last. You are more prepared after writing the complete business plan to write an effective summary.

Ideally, it's a stand-alone document. Often investors will first request only the executive summary in order to evaluate their interest. If there is interest, they will request the complete plan. Alternatively, they could request a pitch presentation plus other data they specifically want to see.

You are introducing your company. As the critical section of your plan, it should be concise, accurate, formal, and serious.

Tell your reader the name of your company, what it is, as in what it will do; how your company will be successful, how it will be managed and where it will be located.

Include highlights of financial information and profit-yielding growth plans in a few paragraphs. While covering key points do not use too much detail, or make the summary too long.

This is a bird's eye view, a quick read to spark interest and captivate the investors. You want to grab the reader's attention, show how interesting, clever and initiative you will be with your business. Put a little meat on those bones.

On the following pages is an Executive Summary from the Small Business Administration. Any form of an executive summary is a <u>summary</u> of your business written at the <u>executive</u> level.

The example of a short summary is in chart form. It does not have to be in this particular page layout, make it your own. However, see how closely it resembles a lean plan.

Section 1: Executive Summary for Pet Grandma

From: https://helpyourpaper.com

Our Mission

Pet Grandma offers superior on-site pet sitting and exercising services for dogs and cats, providing the personal, loving pet care that the owners themselves would provide if they were home. Our team will ensure that pet owners can take business trips or vacations knowing that their pets are in good hands.

The Company and Management

Pet Grandma is headquartered in the City of West Vancouver and incorporated in the Province of British Columbia. The company is owned by partners Pat Simpson and Terry Estelle. Pat has extensive experience in animal care while Terry has worked in sales and marketing for 15 years.

The management of Pet Grandma consists of co-owners Pat Simpson and Terry Estelle. Both partners will be taking hands-on management roles in the company. In addition, we have assembled a board of advisers to provide management expertise. The advisers are:

1. Juliette LeCroix, a partner at LeCroix Accounting

2. Carey Boniface, veterinarian, and partner at Little Tree Animal Care Clinic

3. John Toms, president of Toms Communications Ltd.

Our Services

Our clients are dog and cat owners who choose to leave their pets at home when they travel or who want their pets to have company when their owners are at work. Pet Grandma offers a variety of pet care services, all in the pet's home environment, including:

· Dog walking

· Daily visits

· 24-hour care for days or weeks

· Administration of medications by qualified staff

· Emergency treatment in case of illness (arranged through veterinarians)

· Plant watering

· Mail collection

· Garbage/recycling

Page 1

The Market

Across Canada the pet care business has seen an explosion of growth over the last three years. West Vancouver is an affluent area with a high pet density. Our market research has shown that 9 out of 10 pet owners polled in West Vancouver would prefer to have their pets cared for in their own homes when they travel rather than be kenneled and 6 out of 10 would consider having a pet sitter provide company for their dog when they were at work.

Our Competitive Advantages

· While there are currently eight businesses offering pet sitting in West Vancouver, only three of these offer on-site pet care and none offers "pet visit" services for working pet owners.

· Pet Grandma's marketing strategy is to emphasize the quality of pet care we provide ("a Grandma for your pet!") and the availability of our services. Dog owners who work, for instance, will come home to find happy, friendly companions who have already been exercised and walked rather than demanding whiny animals.

- All pet services will be provided by animal care certified staff.

- All employees are insured and bonded.

Financial Projections

Based on the size of our market and our defined market area, our sales projections for the first year are $340,000. We project a growth rate of 10 percent per year for the first three years.

The salary for each of the co-owners will be $40,000. On startup, we will have six trained staff to provide pet services and expect to hire four more this year once financing is secured. To begin with, co-owner Pat Simpson will be scheduling appointments and coordinating services, but we plan to hire a full-time receptionist this year as well.

Already we have service commitments from over 40 clients and plan to aggressively build our client base through the newspaper, website, social media, and direct mail advertising. The loving on-site professional care that Pet Grandma will provide is sure to appeal to cat and dog owners throughout the West Vancouver area.

Startup Financing Requirements

We are seeking an operating line of $150,000 to finance our first-year growth.

Together, the co-owners have invested $62,000 to meet working capital

requirements.

Page 2

COMPANY DESCRIPTION

Company Insight

Before we get into writing your company description, I want to present some information about slogans, mottos, vision and/or mission statements. The companies used here, as examples, are companies you are familiar with. As a result of their marketing and advertising, you know who they are and what they do.

You also know what problems they solve for consumers. Since your next step is to write your company description, how will you describe it so that people at large will immediately understand why they need it?

You have the name of your company, and you understand the field of the business you are in and the industry. Within the section of company description, start with writing a mission statement.

You may use the mission statement in various places, you do not want it to be too long, but use factual information, especially if you are using numbers. Targets and goals are the best way to describe your mission.

The following pages of company logos and copy are public information. However, never plagiarize.

Defenders of Wildlife: The protection of all native animals and plants in their natural communities.

Amnesty International: To undertake research and action focused on preventing and ending grave abuses of these rights.

Creative Commons develops, supports, and stewards legal and technical infrastructure that maximizes digital creativity, sharing and innovation.

Amazon

To be earth's most customer-centric company; to build a place where people can come to find and discover anything they might want to buy online.

Amazon has combined their mission statement with their vision statement. Visit their site to review.

Apple

Apple is committed to bringing the best personal computing experience to students, educators, creative professionals and consumers around the world through its innovative hardware, software and internet offerings.

Dell

To be the most successful computer company in the world at delivering the best customer experience in markets we serve.

Facebook

To give people the power to share and make the world more open and connected.

Google

Organize the world's (sic) information and make it universally accessible and useful.

Microsoft

Enable people and businesses throughout the world to realize their full potential.

Great, but more of a vision statement don't you think? It's definitely not quantifiable, which is what a vision is?

Skype

Be the fabric of real-time communication on the web.

Twitter

Twitter lists its mission as "a work in progress" as it has yet to be fully developed.

Yahoo!

To be the most essential global internet service for consumers and businesses.

YouTube

Provide fast and easy video access and the ability to share videos frequently.

McDonalds

To be our customers' favorite place and way to eat. Our worldwide operations are aligned around a global strategy called the Plan to Win, which center on an exceptional customer experience – People, Products, Place, Price and Promotion. We are committed to continuously improving our operations and enhancing our customers' experience.

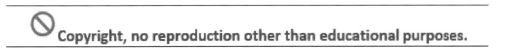

"Uber is evolving the way the world moves. By seamlessly connecting riders to drivers through our apps, we make cities more accessible, opening up more possibilities for riders and more business for drivers."

"Our goal when we created Tesla a decade ago was the same as it is today: to accelerate the advent of sustainable transport by bringing compelling mass-market electric cars to market as soon as possible."

KICKSTARTER

"To help bring creative projects to life."

asana

"To help humanity thrive by enabling all teams to work together effortlessly."

"To enrich people's lives with programmes and services that inform, educate and entertain."

Forbes

"To deliver information on the people, ideas and technologies changing the world to our community of affluent business decision makers."

"To be one of the world's leading producers and providers of entertainment and information, using its portfolio of brands to differentiate its content, services and consumer products."

"To be a company that inspires and fulfills your curiosity."
The largest high-quality content producer for digital media – locally, regionally, nationally and globally (as of 2011).

"Making the best possible ice cream, in the nicest possible way"

The following are company descriptions and public Information. These descriptions include name, contact information, a motto, business description and a mission statement. These may suggest a format for your company description.

Aflac

1932 Wynnton Road Columbus, GA 31999

Slogan / Motto

Aflac insurance policies may help you with those expenses not covered by   your major medical plan.

Description

Aflac is a supplemental insurance company in the U.S. Its main business is into health and life insurance policies that cover special conditions, particularly cancer. Aflac insurance policies help customers with expenses not covered by the medical plan. And unlike other health insurance companies that pay out the money to the doctor or the hospital, Aflac can reimburse the customer so that he is able to control the cash settlement instead.

Mission Statement

To combine aggressive strategic marketing with quality products and services at competitive prices to provide the best insurance value for consumers.

AGCO

AGCO Corporation 4205 River Green Parkway, Duluth, GA, USA 30096

Slogan / Motto

A World of Solutions for your Growing Needs

Description

AGCO is the chief manufacturer and distributor of agricultural equipment such as replacement parts, tractors, hay tools, sprayers, forage equipment and implements. Their brand names include AGCO, Challenger, Fendt, Gleaner, Hesston, Massey Ferguson, RoGator, Spra-Coupe, Sunflower, Terra-Gator, Valtra and White Planters

Mission Statement

Profitable growth through superior customer service, innovation, quality and commitment.

Some of the mission statements in these examples may seem a little long. A few, such as Microsoft and McDonalds, have combined a mission and vision statement together. Definitely have a mission statement. You can have a vision statement or a combination of the two. But clearly state your mission.

If you are using your business plan to obtain financing, the people you are presenting your request to will ask you what they want to know. Questions such as: Where do you see yourself going? How big do you see the business getting? What are your plans for product life cycles?

This could be a sign they haven't read the plan. Or, they have read it and want to see if thinking on your feet matches what you present in the written word. You want to be prepared! You may have left something out, or a point is fuzzy to your audience.

If you are writing a business plan for yourself, write a personal mission statement.

11 ITEMS TO INCLUDE IN YOUR COMPANY DESCRIPTION

The following outlines the information to include in your company description. You want a high-level document since details are covered elsewhere.

1. Company name

The official name of your business. How you registered with your state and county licenses and under what legal structure. For instance, Simon Says, LLC.

2. Business structure

What kind of operation will your business be, and is it a new business or established business:

- Wholesale
- Retail
- Service
- Food
- Manufacturing

3. Legal structure

Make sure you have the proper kind of insurance needed for the structure of your company. You do not have to discuss it here, but consider things like a catastrophe, employee error, damage to the building or office, equipment, etc.

- Sole Proprietor
- Doing Business As (DBA)
- General Partnership, Limited Partnership
- Limited Liability Partnership (LLP)
- Limited Liability Limited Partnership (LLLP)
- Corporation
  - S Corporation, C Corporation
  - Limited Liability Company/Corporation (LLC)
- Nonprofit Corporation
- Limited Liability Company (LLC)
- Trust
- Joint Venture
- Tenants in Common
- Association

4. Ownership/Management

Detail who your principal or key people are and what they will contribute to the success of the business.

5. Location

Where the business is located. It could be an office, a warehouse, a home business, a rented office. Truthfully state where you will be headquartered.

6. Company history

State if yours is an established business and you are requesting funding, or have a plan to increase the scope of your business. What made you want to open your business, and what need do you supply to the marketplace.

7. Mission statement

See discussion at the beginning of this chapter. This is the concise purpose of your business. The mission statement should be placed at the beginning of your business description.

8. Product/Service

To write the text for your business description use only current, reliable data. You are going to have to prove your information in the case of requesting funding. Investors do not invest in perceived risk, estimates, guesswork or assumptions.

If you are not requesting outside funds, the business description should still be accurate and true. You will not be kidding anyone but yourself if you do not use reliable data.

Use footnotes to cite data resources, graphs, charts. Anything that you are using to sell your business idea.

9. Market Analysis

Within the short description, discuss the industry, its present situation and future challenges, possibilities, trends, goals, and the competition.

Speak to various markets within the industry. For instance, toys are typically classified by age groups; clothes for men, women and children by age; coffee, caffeinated or decaf, imported, makeup of the beans; carpet, indoor, outdoor, wool, nylon, acrylic, stain resistant; dog grooming, mobile, by appointment, number of pets per hour, spa treatments, walk-ins; cleaning service, deep clean, move-in move-out clean, weekly clean. You get the idea.

Include in the company description any new products, changes or developments within the industry that may have damaging effects, as well as those that will help your business thrive and grow.

You want to have outlined what is coming down the pike that will help you and how it will affect your business and profits. You must also address any adverse changes and how you will resolve them.

Think from the consumer's point of view. For instance, am I reading a book for a book report or using CliffsNotes? Am I getting my carpets cleaned or renting a machine. Will I do my own yard work, hire someone, or find a kid in the neighborhood.

10. Objectives

What are you going to accomplish today? What can you do right now to get started on your goals? What are your objectives for future growth and resolving issues. Show some true passion for what you are doing and trying to accomplish.

11. Vision Statement

As discussed at the beginning of the chapter, you can have both a mission and a vision statement. It is up to you. But basically, tells how you see the future.

SAMPLE COMPANY DESCRIPTION

Following is a short company description example to show you the required information. This is very brief, and yours will, no doubt, be longer. But, since I cannot write it for you, these are the points to cover.

Our mission is to provide authentic wood-pit high-quality barbecued meats and popular side dishes for a fair price in a clean, fun environment.

(Mission statement)

The Bubba's Bar-B-Que restaurant will be located at 6440 Alafaya Road, Dallas,

(Company name)   *(Company location)*

Texas 73590. The restaurant will be a partnership owned and operated by Jim and Joe Simon.

(Legal structure)   *(Ownership and management)*

We will be a traditional full-service barbecue restaurant serving classic barbecued meat entrees. Meat will be cooked over large, restaurant equipped, wood fire pits. Service will include beer, wine, and soft drinks.

(Business structure-food service)

There is only one other barbecue restaurant within a 10-mile radius in an area of 650,000 people not including 45,000 college students in residence nine months a year. The area includes 99 other restaurants of varying size and product offerings. The extensive shopping center in the area includes movie theaters. The location and restaurant can bear a competitive price range.

(Market analysis)

Our objective is to offer a basic barbecue menu of chicken, beef, and pork. All meats will be smoked for twelve hours over an authentic wood fire pit with a choice of side dishes, soft drinks, beer, and wine. Food is prepared fresh every day, served in a family friendly casual atmosphere. We will operate in a growing neighborhood.

(Objective)

Within three years we plan to open a catering division, complete with mobile fire pits and equipment. At five years, we plan to add a full-service bar with a band, dancing, and additional outdoor patio space.

(Vision statement)

Barbecued meats include ribs, baby back ribs, brisket, hamburgers, pulled pork, and chicken. Included is a choice of two side dishes: pork and beans, coleslaw, green beans, or French fries. All entrees will come with Texas toast and a choice of three different barbecue sauces. Lava cake will be on the menu for dessert.

(Products)

Available from the menu will be large portions of barbecue meats, for example, one pound or two pounds of ribs, chicken or other meat. As well as, quarts or gallons of green beans, pork and beans or coleslaw, and multiple lava cakes. Other weights and sizes of side dishes can be ordered ahead of time.

Service will be provided inside a restaurant building and an adjoining outside patio. Products will be available for order at a drive through window.

(Services)

The restaurant will be open seven days a week.

Monday through Thursday from 11: am – 9 p.m.,

Friday and Saturday from 11 a.m. through 10 p.m.

Sunday from noon through 5 p.m.

This is a new business, so there is no history to be covered. Let's say, for instance, Bubba's is established. Your bar, music, and dancing are an extension to the existing restaurant.

The new extension is what your business plan would be about. That business description section is where you describe the history of the original restaurant then outline the new business extension as a new company description.

DETAIL OF SERVICE OR PRODUCT

This section describes the core of your product or service and explains what you want to achieve.

Topics should include the following elements. However, these examples are short answers to the given question, and only demonstrate the type of information each category should cover. You will write complete answers concerning your business.

What will you be selling?

Barbecued beef, pork and chicken entrees with side orders, soft drinks, beer, and wine.

How will your product or service benefits customers?

Offers clean, friendly dining in a family atmosphere. Provides casual, relaxed dining in a full-service establishment including outdoor dining. Fast service for quick in and out dining. Offers another option to neighborhood dining.

What sets you apart from your competitors?

Authentic wood fire pits. High-quality meats smoked 12 hours. Convenient location. Take out window. Large orders are available for takeout.

Does your product or service have a life cycle?

Yes. Our product will start at the introductory level with the basic restaurant and drive-through window. As awareness and product sales move into the growth stage, we will use revenue and profits to open up a new market and distribution channel with the catering business.

Continuing growth and entering the maturity product life cycle, we will expand our services to include a bar, music, dancing and increased outdoor space. We think that these additions will enable us to run the restaurant as a cash cow and extend this cycle for a very long time.

We will use our knowledge, research, and awareness to implement this new mix of marketing and packaging. Our changes will continue to differentiate us from the competition and allow us our continued profits.

DETAILS OF THE PROBLEM YOU ARE TRYING TO RESOLVE

- Area needs a unique casual alternative food choice.
- People want barbecue but don't want the hassle of firing up a grill and cooking it themselves.
- People want to barbecue but accidentally run out of gas before or during cooking.
- They do not want to deal with canisters of gas or bags of charcoal.
- Bad weather prohibits barbecuing.
- People want barbecue but do not want to/cannot take the time especially on weeknights.
- Every family member wants a different kind of meat entree.

DETAILS OF HOW YOU WILL SOLVE THE PROBLEM

- No need for firing up the home barbecue grills.
- Saves time and eliminates the hassle of gas canisters and charcoal bags.
- Eliminates the inconvenience of bad weather conditions.
- No waiting for the fire to get hot enough.
- No continuous management of fire.
- No running out of gas during cooking not having gas canisters on hand.
- Barbecue available every day of the week.
- Every family member can select their own choice of barbecue entrée.
- Provides take-out service for small and large orders at a fast drive-through window.
- Offering a casual full-service dining restaurant within an easy to reach neighborhood.

COMPETITIVE LANDSCAPE

Within a ten-mile radius, there is only one restaurant dedicated to barbecue products or theme. The immediate area served reaches about 650,000 people, the majority are families.

However, the service area includes a large university; a small college; four apartment complexes, and it is within sight of a large shopping center that includes movie theaters.

Bubba's is the only restaurant dedicated to wood fire pit barbeque; slow smoked for twelve hours

Include all critical information. It can be in paragraph form with or without paragraph headings. Use the structure of your paragraph; first sentence is 'big' point, followed by supporting facts.

Each 'big' point, topic, subject, the idea (whatever you want to call it) may need multiple paragraphs to support it. Just keep using the same structure for each subsequent paragraph.

You don't have to use a lot of big words or technical explanation. Be straightforward and clear in your ideas. It is not a textbook.

PRODUCT LIFE CYCLE (PLC)

Within the business world, product or service sales pass through four levels. This means that sales of product or service follow patterns, and at any time they will be in one of four cycles: introduction, growth, maturity or decline.

Obviously, you first develop your product or service. You are developing your business for a specific target market with the goal of resolving a problem(s).

After you develop your product or service, you are anxious to get it out into the marketplace. Sounds good so far. The various cycles are where big changes come in to drive your business marketing plan.

The big news for your sales is that products have an innate PLC. Therefore, you cannot stay static. You will need appropriate marketing plans for each level your product goes through.

If this sounds familiar, it should. Think how many times I have said that your plan is not static, it has to evolve, never sit still. You will have to adjust your marketing plan for each cycle.

This is how the PLC helps to direct your company.

INTRODUCTION STAGE

This is a big expense level. If you are writing a plan to obtain financing, this is the core piece. This is where you will start high financial investments and planning.

At this stage you are new in the market. Therefore, demand and sales are low, and expenses are high. If you have an established business and are writing a plan for expansion or adding new products this element still needs to be discussed.

Here is how the two compare:

- If your company is **established** and you are improving what you already have, or your product does something totally new or adds new technology, you can command a higher price. This allows you to recover your Research and Development (R&D) expenses more quickly.

A good example that everyone can relate to is the cost of prescription drugs. When a new drug hits the marketplace, it is at a very high price. The drug companies have to recover the multi-million dollars spent to develop the drug.

$$\$\$\$\$\$\$\$\$\$\$\$\$\$\$\$\$\$\$$$

The higher price, which lasts until the R&D expenses have been recovered, will drop at a much far-out future date. The price will also drop due to competition or new formulas or upgrades. Then the cycle starts again, R&D of new formulas, FDA approval, market push, high prices, and so on.

Other examples are the first computers and software, cell phones, calculators, etc. As R&D is recuperated the companies and manufacturers continue to build the next big thing. The next big thing quickly becomes outdated, and the cycle continues.

With established businesses such as these, there are people who are considered early adopters. They have already bought into the product, are hooked for whatever reason and will pay for upgrades. This group is not as price sensitive as when first starting out with a product.

Your job at this point is having the product with a dynamic marketing plan aimed at your target market. You will need to convince investors or internal company gate-keepers to pay for the high development and promotional costs. In other words, a business plan

- In the case of a **new business**, your product may have to be tried by consumers before they understand the value. You are looking at promotional costs which may have to include reduced introductory pricing to get attention.

It may also be necessary to give away free samples if it would fit in with your product. You might consider something like a punch card where the first product or use of service is at an introductory price. Subsequent uses or purchases after the first could reward the consumer with a free product or service.

You have seen this type of promotion in the marketplace, probably even used it. This particular example may not fit in with you, your product or target market. But, get creative.

If your product is a service, you experience the development costs in products, location(s), possible training, transportation, equipment, etc.

You need an aggressive marketing plan along with the costs of possible reduced introductory prices, giveaways or rewards for using your service.

GROWTH STAGE

As you see your business or service take off and grow, you will be able to increase service locations, for instance, or offer expanded services. As for the product, you will be able to ramp up production. This means that this growth stage brings your costs down and allows you to reinvest some revenue into new distribution channels and new markets.

If you are at the growth stage, you should be capitalizing on your product or service and start your plans for improvements and expansion. Keep your eye on any competition, because any good, money making idea can be stolen, thereby, reducing your market share.

MATURITY PHASE

This product stage is also known as the cash cow because it is the phase where you make the most money without the large initial investment type of promotion and advertising. You hold awareness of your product or service, your loans or R&D expenses are paid off. However, you probably have more competition chewing at your target market.

You do have a couple of options at this point. You could lower the price of your product or service to stay competitive and relevant. That depends on the marketplace and how you emotionally feel about that. You need to do a lot of research on the topic and find out what goes on when you drop your prices.

The second option is to reinvent yourself. Much like the example of Bubba's Bar-B-Que, moving into the maturity PLC, they plan to add a bar, music, and dancing. Basically, repackaging themselves and opening up a new market and promotion channels.

They had added catering to their line-up in the growth stage which helped them to run profitably and differentiate themselves from the competition in the marketplace and to stay new and relevant.

This is the phase where you stand to make the most money. Put some of it back into the business. Get your business plan out, and put your next steps into action. This is a good example of showing you how your business evolves and how your business plan is a growing, changing evolving document.

DECLINE PHASE

The overall cost for running the business is as low as it will ever be in this phase. Here, again, you have some options. One, lower your prices to stay competitive and keep the business coming in if you have not already. However, if you have added new products or services at the various PLC stages all of the product life cycles will be varied and enable you to cover the drop-in demand for the product or service you started with.

- Go back and think about technology, or even soft drinks and cars. These guys have been around a long time and are not going anywhere. What is the biggest thing they have done? Reinvent.

- You will always know which stage of PLC your product or service is in; your sales numbers are the clue. During a drop-in business and profits, you can do one of two things. You can wait it out, or you can put more money into promotion and other marketing to prolong the product/service life.

- It is very tricky because if you give up and stop offering your services or cut down, stop marketing and reduce production of your product. Your business then becomes the PLC not stated anywhere, the self-fulfilling end.

MARKET ANALYSIS

As important as offering a specific product or service, you have to detail who you will market and sell to. The first thing to do is describe your market. Not just who you are selling to, but how many are there, and who else is doing the same thing as you want to do.

That is what market analysis is. We need to talk about the basics of market segmentation, then discuss the questions you will need to answer in this section.

Evaluation of the Market

Your market is not everyone. Therefore, your market research and analysis have the goal of identifying your market segments. A segment is a group of people within your market that will buy your product or service. Each of the segments is your target market.

Out of everyone, there are specific groups that will buy your product or service. In the example of Bubba's, the market segments are:

1. Families

2. Couples

3. Groups of friends

4. Individuals

Each segment will have a percentage of who dines out, where, when, and why. Are they looking for a specific kind of food, theme, atmosphere or convenience of location? Will they use the drive-through window? What is the average age and the average amount of the ticket?

A good business plan not only identifies the target market, but it also breaks it down into segments and includes data showing how fast each will grow from many angles. Here is the methodology:

TAM: Total Available Market. How big is the entire market that you could provide product or service to? For instance, the entire city Bubba's is located in has a population of three million people.

SAM: Segmented Available Market. The group you will target from the TAM data. For instance, Bubba's will be on the east side of the main county of the city. That area of town's population is 650,000 people plus 45,000 college students who are in residence nine months a year.

SOM: Share of Market. This subset is who you could actually reach in the first year or so of being in business. This number is extrapolated from SAM. How many of those 650,000 people and the 45,000 college students can you reach and convince to spend their money on your product?

While you are putting together the numbers and size of your market segments, also research the potential growth of each. Does the college market segment basically stay the same year to year? How many students remain in the area? How fast is the target area of 650,000 growing per year, in percentages? Is it in decline?

The growth or decline must be in relation to the population of the market segment. For instance, the population of the 650,000-person area may be growing 3% a year. What are those changes and why are they happening? Are more families appearing in the mix; a higher number of teenagers or millennials; retired people; high salaries, lower; what is the trend of the neighborhoods?

See the Appendix for some various sources of data. These and other sources will help you gather information on your market analysis.

Research topics to visit, such as:

- Bubba's is in a residential neighborhood, great schools and a mix of salary ranges. Address what the salary levels are. Number of schools, grade levels, attendance.

- There are apartment complexes. What kind, who lives there, economic view, children, students, etc.

- Level of various ethnics in the entire area. For example, will Orientals eat barbeque? Is this a pocket of ethnicity? Much like a Little Italy or Little Viet Nam?

- Single family homes. Price range, number, and age of homes. Turnover of the real estate, etc.

- Large shopping area. How many restaurants, what type; clothing or grocery stores, what audience; movie theaters, how many?

- Traffic distribution system. Close to main arteries, easy access for others in the city, the main drag?

- What other businesses are in the area? Is there an airport, hotels, hospitals?

- Reaching your market and creating profits is limited by all the other businesses in the industry. You have to find ways to overcome those limits.

EVALUATION OF THE COMPETITION

If you are opening a restaurant, what other and how many restaurants are in your marketing area? What are the sizes, are they a chain, what are the themes, what are the foods served and what audience to they attract? What are their hours, do they deliver?

If you want a shop to sell clothes, whose clothes are you selling? Just baby, just women or men, teenagers, sports, family? Who are the competitors? For instance, how well would a boutique shop do against a Kohl's or Target? Would the neighborhood support it, or would word of mouth? Are you different enough and how?

When you discuss the competition, talk about who is offering the same services or providing the same products. Other businesses want to solve your customer's problems, too. How is what you are going to offer better? What is your advantage? Discuss how, in your environment, you will create a better, more successful business. This is also called the value proposition.

Business people typically use a competitor matrix to list competitors and how they stack up against themselves. Build your matrix using excel if it will be a long comparison chart. If not, or if you prefer, just build it in chart form in Word.

List you and your competitors down the left side. This is column one. Build additional columns next to it listing each of the competitor's features.

Name	Casual or Theme	Late hrs. Reg. Hours	7 Days or Days Open	Lit Parking Lot	Easy in-out Access	Street View or any View
Bubba's						
Chili's						
Fridays						
Mac Grill						
MacDonald						
Panera Bread						
Red Lobster						

Shake and Steak						

This is just a slice of an example. Use multiple columns for every amenity and as many competitors as possible. Have layout and printing done professionally if conceivable. Regardless of size, the chart must be professional for a business plan presented to investors.

EVALUATION OF MARKET CHARACTERISTICS

As part of an industry, your readers, investors, need to understand the market of your industry. Not everyone knows about the carpet or home improvement industry, food or technology industries. But, you need to, and you have to explain it clearly, knowledgeably and concisely.

Discuss a little of the history of the industry, profitability and the health of the overall industry. Think about steel. You are probably not going into that industry but think about the history you could write. From the industrial revolution to foreign trade and tariffs. You don't have to write a book, but put together several paragraphs or a timeline pointing out the milestones.

What are the trends? For instance, do people prefer marble, tile and wood floors instead of wall to wall carpet in every room? Why, who are these people, and what is their price point? People dress more casually today than in the past. Where is that trend/style now, why did it change, will it continue, and why?

Sports equipment changes, cooking trends, even the automobiles that we own. Changes can be due to changes in the market such as availability and/or imports, tariffs, or changes in trends. Life changes affect a product or service, for instance, aging, marriage, children, college, retirement, and so on.

You may be thinking that these descriptions and history are too big or too much for you, simply extend the application, extrapolate.

For instance, sports equipment. The history of biking is manageable. And, your little shop could handle repairs of the new and/or foreign bikes. Performance bikes, road, mountain, carbon fiber, Bianchi, Schwinn, and high-tech components. Whatever you want to target, and possibly include biking groups and biking excursions.

Here is another simpler example. A sports shoe or equipment store could offer custom orthodontics that are at sky-rocket prices at podiatrists. You have heard of diving goggles with prescription lenses. Where would a diver find those? Do you have a dive shop? Partner with local eye doctors. Are you selling surfboards, excursions, lessons?

Another example. What trends have the auto and auto repair industries gone through? What is up ahead? The new high-tech cars need specific technical training for repairs. Cameras on the four sides may be damaged with just a bump to the car. Repairs for the future high-tech automobiles is going to be expensive.

It is going to be a long time before you can buy parts for this sensitive equipment on Amazon or a parts department or store. Maybe you could be the local service professional person for repairs listed on Amazon.

All of the new technology like cameras, devices, giggles, and gaggles' repairs will be extremely high and extremely profitable. Beware of products that are cheap to replace instead of repair.

The kind of in-depth facts and data I am telling you to obtain and clearly state is the data that proves there is a market for your product or service. It is also the basis of your forecasted sales, states that there is a future, and how far can you take your expertise.

The facts and data determine the size of your business and practically write your marketing plan for you. This research identifies your financial needs and anticipated profits.

MARKETING AND ADVERTISING

Detailing your marketing and advertising plans should be done by product lifecycle. Know each cycle, the benefits, changes, types, and channels of advertising you will use.

For instance, in the introductory stage, most of your focus will be on building brand awareness. You may be using free samples, but your big investments will be made in advertising and digital marketing. You must engage as many people as possible to create demand through promotion.

In the growth stage, most businesses spend more on brand equity and preference. More dollars are spent on the advertising and digital content than were spent in the introduction phase. More money should be coming in, justifying the expense, and public relations should support the advertising.

In the maturity life cycle, the marketing and advertising focus shifts to capturing the competitors' market share by getting customers to be brand loyal to you. Also, the maturity stage can be an introductory stage for various new lines, products, services you add to your business.

It becomes harder to acquire new customers. Therefore, you have to keep sales from slipping by keeping existing customers satisfied. Retain loyal customers with ongoing campaigns to get feedback through email and newsletters. Use these and other channels of promotion to provide information that enhances the benefits of your product or service.

Revisit Bubba's plan to see the owners' plans for expansion during maturity to capture a new and additional market. Their maturity expansions become an introductory product/service, and the cycle starts over for those expansions.

Extend the maturity stage as long as possible. Use reward programs, fresh themes in your marketing, and show your product in a new way. Change and switch out the media you use.

This is especially important in the decline phase. Find new ways to look at or use your product. The main focus will be on the brand image. You will be spending more time on publicity and public relations in this phase.

The marketing and advertising section of your plan will employ tactics such as these. Detail what marketing and advertising strategy you will use, when, how, and how it fits into your plan to successfully reach your target market.

THE MANAGEMENT PLAN

This section describes your management team and staff, and how business ownership is structured. Readers want to know who is on your team, their skills, and what they can contribute to the bottom line.

Break this section into four parts:

1. Ownership Structure
2. Internal Management
3. External Management
4. Human Resources Needs

Ownership

This is the legal structure of your business. It has been discussed in other parts of the plan, but review it here in this section. You want to clearly define who holds what percent ownership in the company.

Internal Management

Following are the main business management categories, use the ones pertinent to your business or service.

- Sales
- Marketing
- Administration
- Production
- Human Resources
- Research and Development

Identify the person/people who have the responsibility for each category, their skills, and include their resumes. It is not necessary to have one person per category, for instance, one key person can fill many roles.

You, for example, are sales, marketing, and production. Your partner, or family member, could be human resources and administration. Identify key people. The bigger your company, the more key people and categories. Deduce what and who you need by the business you are in, and the size of business you are going to start-up. You may start-up with a few people and add others along the way.

This internal management plan results in your management team outline. Discuss salary, benefits profit-sharing and non-compete agreements.

External Management

External management are your internal management's back-up. You may have a use for:

1. Professional Services:

- Accountants
- Bankers
- Lawyers
- IT Consultants (you may just need the Geek Squad, but list it)
- Business consultants

2. An Advisory Board

Set one up, no matter the size of your business. A group of friends, a group of other small business people, retired execs, vendors. A think-tank type of situation that could give advice and/or spark ideas. Anything to help make the business a success.

Human Resources Needs

Start with the bottom line. This section holds a lot of interest for readers, as employees represent the highest overhead line item. Number and name the employees you will need, their skills, and how much it will cost.

Then discuss how you will meet those HR needs. Will it be through independent contractors, freelancers, part-time employees, a mix, or a schedule of hiring a few along the way as needed? Having listed the type of employee(s) calculate labor costs.

Depending on your type of business, here is an example. Reason it out to match your business or service:

> 1 employee can serve 100 customers
> You forecast 1000 customers the first year
> You need 10 employees
> At what milestones do you add employees?

Think in restaurant terms for wait staff:

> 1 employee can service 10 tables/ 4-top, per night/day
> You forecast 80 tables for tonight
> You need 8 wait staff (does not include any other staff)

Your labor costs, therefore, are the total amount of salaries you are paying for all employees, plus Workers' Compensation Insurance, and benefits, such as medical/dental.

Other costs to add to HR needs are staff recruitment and training.

While you may be the only employee to start, or you and your partner, still include this section on HR to prove that you have thought about future staffing needs and that you will have HR policies in place. Talk about your future needs, show off your knowledge.

OPERATING PLAN

The operating plan describes the physical necessities of your business's operation. Where will your business be located, what equipment and what facilities are needed?

You may also have inventory requirements, how much stock will you need at any one time, for how long and under what conditions? Explain the supplier and manufacturer chain as well.

Stay focused on the bottom line. An operating plan is an outline of capital and expense requirements needed to run your business on a daily basis. You have two topics to discuss. The Stage of Development and the Production Process.

While I am not running your business, and cannot address detail for any of the following, I can outline what these two topics entail. As a small business owner study how each detail applies to your business, and cover it suitably.

STAGE OF DEVELOPMENT

An outline, basically, of what have you done to date to get your business up and running.

- What is the production workflow
- How will your product or service be made
- How will it be distributed
- What are potential problems, for instance, the shutdown of equipment, employee accidents
- How will you handle risk, for example, hazardous materials, storm damage
- Show your knowledge of local, regional, and national standards and regulations by industry organization and how you are complying
- Discuss supply chains
- Who are the vendors, their prices, terms and conditions, and your alternative suppliers
- How are you meeting quality control
- What QC measures exist
- Are you pursuing or do you hold any QC certifications

PRODUCTION PROCESS

This is where you discuss the details of your day-to-day operations.
- General

Chart or outline of your day-to-day operations. Days and hours of operation, etc.

- Physical

  Do you have a physical plant/facility? Give size and location, drawings, lease agreements, real estate appraisals. Your business and plan may be much simpler. Maybe you just need a place to store inventory. No matter the size, write it up. For instance, a warehouse, maybe even just a storage locker. Offer size, location, rent. What you will store in there, etc.

- Equipment

  What equipment do you need, its worth, its cost, and what financial arrangements you have to buy/lease it

- Assets

  Do you have any land, buildings, inventory, furniture, equipment or vehicles? Include the value of each asset and legal description

- Special requirements

  Are there any water or power needs? Do you need drainage, ventilation? What have you done regarding permissions, zoning approvals, etc?

- Materials

  Where will you get your materials to make your product, who are the suppliers, and what are the terms you have with your suppliers

- Production

  How long does it take to produce a unit, frame of production?

- Inventory

  What do you need to keep in inventory, how will you track inventory

- Feasibility

  Details of product testing, price and prototype testing

- Cost

  Product cost estimates

The best part is that once you have worked through this business plan section, you will have a detailed operations plan to show the readers of your business plan, plus a convenient list of what needs to be done next to make your business succeed.

THE FINANCIAL PLAN

The financial plan comes at the end of the business plan, but it is the section that will determine if your plan is viable or not, and is the major component in attracting investors.

As a small business owner, you may or may not need an accountant, but if you are not familiar with financial statements and balance sheets, it would be beneficial to have one.

The financial plan consists of several financial statements.

INCOME STATEMENT

Also called a profit and loss statement (P&L), this is a chart-form summary of your company's P&L for any given period of time. An income statement is typically prepared on a monthly basis, then a quarterly and annual view and comparison. It begins with your revenue, followed by costs section which includes labor and materials. Finally, the last section is operating and overhead, arriving at your net profit.

Here is an example from: Business Town

https://businesstown.com/articles/how-to-create-an-income-statement-for-your-small-business/

Income Statement For Crest Shoe Company Inc.

For Year Ending 12/31/00

Sales	
Gross Sales	$1,139,437
Less Returns	$1,805
Net Sales	$1,137,632
Cost of Goods Sold	
Materials	$47,036
Contract Manufacturing	$247,950
Licensing Payments	$76,387
Total Cost of Goods Sold	$371,373
Gross Profit	$766,259
Operating Expenses	
MARKETING & SALES	
Sales & Mktg Salaries	$137,243
Collateral & Promotions	$13,381
Advertising	$27,313

Income Statement For Crest Shoe Company Inc.

Other Sales & Mkt Costs	$3,412
Total Marketing & Sales Expenses	$181,349
GENERAL & ADMINISTRATIVE	
Office Salaries	$115,823
Rent	$49,315
Utilities	$17,384
Depreciation	$11,939
Other Overhead Costs	$28,875
Total General & Administrative	$223,336
Total Operating Expenses	$404,685
Net Income Before Taxes	$361,574
Taxes	$123,862
Net Income	$237,712

CASH FLOW PROJECTION

A supply of available cash is your daily lifeline. Can you meet day-to-day expenses, deal with emergencies or support a growth burst? Often, a company can show a profit but has no ready cash. A cash flow chart projects your expenses and income.

This sample is provided by Accounting Simplified

Balance sheet for XYZ business on the 31st of December 2010	$	$
ASSETS		
Non-current assets		2,150,000
Land and buildings	2,000,000	
Furniture	12,000	
Machinery	18,000	
Investments	120,000	
Current assets		10,000
Inventory	1,000	
Debtors / receivables	3,200	
Bank and cash	5,800	
TOTAL ASSETS		2,160,000
EQUITY AND LIABILITIES		
Owner's equity		1,700,000
Capital	1,700,000	
Non-current liabilities		440,000
10% Loan	440,000	
Current liabilities		20,000
Creditors / payables	20,000	
TOTAL EQUITY AND LIABILITIES		2,160,000

BREAK-EVEN ANALYSIS

Use the information you have put together from your financials and develop a break-even excel worksheet, or any other software spreadsheet. Investors are going to want to know how long it will take, and how much money you will spend to get to the break-even point.

In addition to making your case for a business loan, a break-even analysis helps you to price more efficiently, and determine profit points for various products or services.

Break-even is when your profits are equal to your costs. Anything above that is net profit.

REQUEST FOR FUNDING

WHAT TO INCLUDE IN YOUR FUNDING REQUEST

There are several ways of looking at a funding request. You are a new start-up, you are adding to an established business. The investor may have invested in the first stage of your start-up, has been paid back, and now you are asking for funding to add to that existing business.

1. A summary of the business. This is already provided in your business plan. However, if you have chosen to submit a lean plan, or a stand-alone request, explain what the company is, where, product or service, and who your customers are. Include the legal structure, names of principals, key staff, and your business accomplishments and successes to date.

   Give lenders a recap. Sometimes, only the Funding Request will be required.

2. How much money are you requesting? In terms of cash, how much do you need now, is this the first part of your start-up/growth plan funding, and how much more money do you plan to request over what period of time.

Develop a timeline. The Small Business Administration recommends thinking as far ahead as five years. In today's market, that is a long time to estimate.

One year of concrete numbers reasoned over a total of three years is sufficient. If investors want more information, they will ask for it.

State the kind of funding you are looking for. Do you want a loan, investment, and what terms are you requesting? Develop different versions of this request for different types of funding.

3. How much money do you need? State dollars you need now, and dollars for the future.

4. What will the money be used for? In the case of your business plan, the money is to start-up and run the new business, and fund it through profit making. Various other uses, depending on your situation, could be to pay-off other high-interest loans, buy more space or equipment, another company, expand advertising, even hiring more staff. Each use must be clearly outlined, with accurate dollar amounts to be used for each.

5. Financial information, and current situation. This request is the heart of your financial information in your plan. If you are established and adding to your business, include historical data such as all of your financial statements, for the last three years.

If funding is for collateral, document what you are using. Have you or others made investments, is there stock equity? Detail all investor funds, and any loans you will be paying off.

In the case of your small, new business, more than likely you have no collateral. You are asking them to fund a business based on future forecasts. Your business plan gives the data they need, but here you need to summarize how you will pay the debt, what kind of ROI are you offering, what is a planned exit plan if needed.

Investors want a maximum return at low risk, an exit strategy if things fall apart, and a plan if they want to cash out at a later date. Do you plan on going public, and address anything that could hinder your ability to repay?

6. Repayment schedule. Outline how you plan to repay any loan; however, the lenders more than likely will let you know what they expect. Tell them if you are planning to sell the business at some point, relocation or buyout.
Additionally, how they exit, or buyout.

REMINDERS FOR WRITING YOUR FUNDING REQUEST

- Tailor your funding request to each financial source. Lenders and investors need different information.
- Keep your funding sources in mind. Each will have different requirement, accommodate them, do research, and address that information in your request.
- As for enough to keep the business going.
- Write in plain English, no acronyms or jargon
- Keep your project focused and do not commit to other plans or projects you cannot deliver.

- Remain specific, do not talk in generalities. For instance, 'we are going to have a shop to repair bikes' or 'we are going to wash cars.' That is not a plan, is it?
- Focus your request on the investor's priorities. Provide all documentation asked for, and all additional information/data requested.
- Present evidence of need for your business.
- Meet deadlines, be on time, dress appropriately.
- Keep your budget specific, and do not include non-specific items in the budget.
- Apply to one investor at a time. Do not put yourself in the damaging position of having to turn an investor down because of a better deal, or you chose the first investor that responded.

WRITING YOUR LETTER OF APPLICATION

- An investor or bank may have their own application. Get a copy ahead of time and have it completed and in your business plan prior to any meeting.
- Use your company headed paper. Design it in Word or have a freelancer mock it up.
- Address your letter to the named contact(s) of the investing group you are applying to.

Logo, if you have it

Your name and role

Your organization's name

Address

Date

Recipient's name

Job title

Organization

Full Address

Dear Mr. Hope You Like Us:

Bubba's Bar-B-Que Application for Restaurant Funding

I (We) are making an application for $100,000 to start-up and run my (our new restaurant, Bubba's Bar-B-Que.

(Short description of your plan; very short)

(Why you want to start your business up)

How you will start it up)

(What you are providing)

(Shortly what you will use the money for)

I (We formally adopted our Constitution/Policy/Guidelines/Working Rules (Whatever you have that shows how you are protecting your brand and company image)

(What you have done so far, even if just looking into licensing, zoning, some basics. Any research; not the specifics just that you have research the market, locations.)

I (We) are requesting an audience with you to investigate funding (loan) possibilities.

Thank you, in advance, for your consideration. I am looking forward to your phone call.

Yours sincerely,

Your full name, Title

Another idea, courtesy of: The Balance small business
https://www.thebalancesmb.com/steps-to-write-a-business-plan-1794230

[DATE]

[NAME]

[ADDRESS]

[ADDRESS]

RE: Financial Funding Proposal

MISSION STATEMENT:

HISTORY:

POPULATION SERVICING:

OVERVIEW OF CURRENT SITUATION:

ANY LOAN HISTORY:

STATEMENT OF NEED:

OBJECTIVES:

EVALUATION, FUNDING MANAGEMENT, AND PLANNING:

BOARD OF DIRECTORS:

BUDGET:

LIST OF EXPENSES AND COSTS FOR MY NEW COMPANY FUNDING PROPOSAL

Expenses	Estimated Amount
Operations	[DOLLAR AMOUNT]
Travel	[DOLLAR AMOUNT]
Supplies	[DOLLAR AMOUNT]
Technology	[DOLLAR AMOUNT]
Utilizes	[DOLLAR AMOUNT]
Rent	[DOLLAR AMOUNT]

Shipping/Delivery	[DOLLAR AMOUNT]
[NAME OF EXPENSE]	[DOLLAR AMOUNT]
[NAME OF EXPENSE]	[DOLLAR AMOUNT]
[NAME OF EXPENSE]	[DOLLAR AMOUNT]
[NAME OF EXPENSE]	[DOLLAR AMOUNT]
[NAME OF EXPENSE]	[DOLLAR AMOUNT]
[NAME OF EXPENSE]	[DOLLAR AMOUNT]

[NAME OF ORGANIZATION]

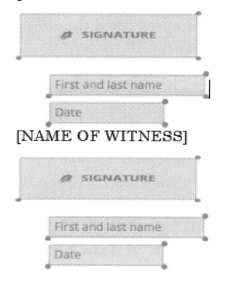

[NAME OF WITNESS]

SUMMARY

How would you plan a trip without a final destination, or a planned route and an iffy mode of transportation? That is exactly what you are doing if you try to start a business without a business plan.

You have more information than that to drive to the grocery store for a gallon of milk.

- You provide food and nourishment for your children.

- Your children need milk for their cereal in the morning.

- You have to go to the store before their breakfast time in the morning to get milk. There is no time with the family's morning rush to run an errand before breakfast. They are young children and insist on their Dinosaurs Crunch in the morning. Nothing else will do.

- You know which store you are going to, based on location, convenience, price, availability, open hours.

- You have to decide how to get there.

  1. You will drive your car. 'Do I have enough gas or do I need to fill up?'

  2. You will ride a bike. 'Is it still light enough or do I have a light?'

3. You will walk. 'Is it close enough, light enough outside?'

4. Do you need a ride from a friend, neighbor, family member? Adjustment: 'Is anyone available?'

5. You may have to send someone else. Adjustment: 'Who, when how?'

6. Do you manage the household and are able to take the children out for breakfast after everyone else leaves? Adjustment: 'Is it too late in the morning to do that, or will they cry all morning?'

- Resolve adjustments to any transportation issues above.

- What if there is inclement weather?

- Resolve adjustments to accommodate the weather.

- If the weather prohibits traveling to the store, how will you resolve the problem?
  Do without
  Go in the morning
  Borrow from neighbor

- In good weather, drive, walk, ride to the store.

- Park, lean bike at a storefront or get dropped off.

- Walk into the front doors.

- Walk to the milk compartment. You may be aware, or not that milk is found at the back of stores for marketing reasons. So, you know where to look.
- Pick up the milk in the brand, container size and price point you need.

- Go to the checkout counter, wait your turn if there is a line.

- Pay for your purchase with cash or your debit card.

- Decide on a bag or no bag and is plastic bag OK.

- Walk to your mode of transportation or turn your body towards your house.

- Ride, drive, walk back home.

- Take the milk container out of the bag, and/or wipe off any moisture.

- Put the milk in the refrigerator.

Job done.

BUSINESS PLAN TEMPLATES

Since you are reading this page, I can safely assume, you read the entire book and have an understanding of all the basics of a typical business plan and all of its components.

Some of you might still need more help in writing a business plan; I can understand that. Those of you that want more help to write your plan, my advice is to use a template. As long as you understand what a business plan and all of its inner workings are, it will be easier for you to work with a template and I am sure if you spend a couple of hours, you will be able to have a plan ready.

Now the big question is where you might get templates right? Well, if you are using Microsoft Word, then you can download many Business Plan templates directly from the Microsoft Office website. Follow this link below, but in the event when this link may change, just type "Microsoft Word Business Plan Templates" in Google, and you will get the updated link.

https://templates.office.com/en-US/Business-plan-TM03843660

Don't worry, it is free, and best of all it is the actual template where all you have to do is fill in the blanks, each section even tells you what and how to fill each of them out. This template will even generate all the bar graphs, charts, and financial data sheets as long as you enter the financial numbers.

You can add your own logo, business name, address, and slogan and customize it any way you want.

Don't spend your hard earn money buying business plan templates, when the best is available for free.

Here is a link to another 10 Free Business Plan Templates from Inc. Magazine.

https://www.inc.com/larry-kim/top-10-business-plan-templates-you-can-download-free.html

Here is a screenshot of the Microsoft Business Plan Template.

replace with
LOGO

[Business Plan Title]

[Business Plan Subtitle]

Table of Contents

LAST WORDS

I know the above is not a business plan. But it's a step by step plan for buying milk via a quick run to the store.

It answers what, when, where, who, why, and how.

Keep details and each step in mind when writing your business plan. It is important to review and revise your plan. Remember that your plan is never finished. It is not a static document.

There is a lot of information in this book. I hope it helps. I hope you will use it. I hope you will read it several times. Hopefully, I was able to give you a good general overview of a solid business plan, and it should be crafted, created and written

I wanted to thank you for buying my book; I am neither a professional writer nor an author, but someone who has a passion for growing businesses to huge success.

In this book, I wanted to share my knowledge with you, as I know there are many people who share the same passion and drive as I do. So, this book is entirely dedicated to YOU, my readers.

Despite my best effort to make this book error free, if you happen to find any errors, I want to ask for your forgiveness ahead of time.

Just remember, my writing skills may not be best, but the knowledge I share here is pure and honest.

If you thought I added some value and shared some valuable information that you can use, please take a minute and post a review on wherever you bought this book from. This will mean the world to me. Thank you so much!!

Lastly, I wanted to thank my wife Natalie and my brother Rob for all their help and support throughout this book, without them, this book would not have been possible.

If you need to get in touch with me for any reason, please feel free to email me at cstoreworld@gmail.com

Thank you once again and Good luck with your new business!

APPENDIX

Data and Statistics:

Https://statista.com/topics/760/united-states

Https://bea.gov/ (US Bureau of Economic Analysis)

Https:www.bls.gov/ (US Bureau of Labor Statistics)

Htpps://www.esa.gov/

Htpps://smallbusinessadministration.com

Https://www.usa.gov/statistics (Includes an industry portal)

Https://www.worldpopulationreview.com

Https://www.census.gov

Https://www.infoplease.com/us/us-states-maps-states

https://templates.office.com/en-US/Business-plan-TM03843660

https://www.inc.com/larry-kim/top-10-business-plan-templates-you-can-download-free.html

All forms and definitions from the web are cited with the text. These are used only to give you ideas about various formats.

Made in the USA
Columbia, SC
07 January 2021